50 Flavorful Gluten-Free Dinners Recipes

By: Kelly Johnson

Table of Contents

- Lemon Herb Chicken with Roasted Vegetables
- Quinoa Stuffed Bell Peppers
- Gluten-Free Chicken Alfredo
- Zucchini Noodles with Pesto Chicken
- Sweet Potato and Black Bean Enchiladas
- Grilled Salmon with Mango Salsa
- Spaghetti Squash Primavera
- Beef and Vegetable Stir-Fry
- Chicken Parmesan with Gluten-Free Breadcrumbs
- Eggplant Parmesan
- Baked Lemon Garlic Shrimp
- Gluten-Free Meatballs with Marinara
- Grilled Steak with Avocado Salsa
- Cauliflower Fried Rice
- Spaghetti with Ground Turkey and Tomato Sauce
- Grilled Portobello Mushrooms with Balsamic Glaze
- Gluten-Free Chicken and Rice Casserole
- Sweet Potato Gnocchi
- Spicy Shrimp Tacos with Lime Crema
- Stuffed Acorn Squash with Quinoa and Cranberries
- Lemon Dill Baked Cod
- Gluten-Free Beef and Broccoli Stir-Fry
- Thai Peanut Chicken Stir-Fry
- Baked Chicken Thighs with Garlic and Herb
- Gluten-Free Lasagna with Zucchini Noodles
- Roasted Vegetable and Chickpea Buddha Bowl
- Salmon and Avocado Rice Bowl
- Cauliflower and Chickpea Curry
- Grilled Chicken with Greek Salad
- Eggplant and Spinach Stuffed Chicken
- Grilled Shrimp Skewers with Garlic and Lemon
- Butternut Squash and Spinach Risotto
- Gluten-Free Shrimp Scampi
- Chicken and Vegetable Skewers
- Spaghetti with Gluten-Free Meat Sauce

- Baked Parmesan Crusted Tilapia
- Gluten-Free Beef Tacos with Avocado
- Sweet Potato and Kale Salad
- Grilled Veggie and Hummus Wrap
- Lemon Garlic Chicken with Quinoa
- Mediterranean Chicken Bowl
- Black Bean and Corn Quinoa Salad
- Zucchini and Ground Turkey Lasagna
- Sweet Chili Chicken with Vegetables
- Shrimp and Grits
- Gluten-Free Chicken Enchilada Casserole
- Veggie and Quinoa Stir-Fry
- Spaghetti with Gluten-Free Carbonara
- Baked Tilapia with Herb Butter
- Gluten-Free Stuffed Peppers with Ground Beef

Lemon Herb Chicken with Roasted Vegetables

Ingredients

- 4 boneless, skinless chicken breasts
- 1 lemon (zested and juiced)
- 2 tbsp olive oil
- 3 garlic cloves, minced
- 1 tsp dried thyme
- 1 tsp dried rosemary
- Salt and pepper, to taste
- 2 cups baby potatoes, halved
- 2 cups carrots, sliced
- 1 bell pepper, chopped
- 1 zucchini, chopped

Instructions

1. **Marinate the Chicken:**
   - In a bowl, combine lemon juice, lemon zest, olive oil, minced garlic, thyme, rosemary, salt, and pepper.
   - Add the chicken breasts and coat them well with the marinade. Let it marinate for at least 30 minutes or overnight in the refrigerator.
2. **Roast the Vegetables:**
   - Preheat the oven to 400°F (200°C).
   - Toss the potatoes, carrots, bell pepper, and zucchini with olive oil, salt, and pepper. Spread them in a single layer on a baking sheet.
   - Roast for 25-30 minutes, turning once until tender and lightly browned.
3. **Cook the Chicken:**
   - Heat a grill or skillet over medium-high heat. Cook the marinated chicken for 6-7 minutes per side or until fully cooked.
4. **Serve:**
   - Plate the roasted vegetables and top with the grilled lemon herb chicken. Garnish with fresh herbs if desired.

Quinoa Stuffed Bell Peppers

Ingredients

- 4 bell peppers (red, yellow, or orange)
- 1 cup quinoa
- 2 cups vegetable broth or water
- 1 tbsp olive oil
- 1 small onion, diced
- 2 garlic cloves, minced
- 1 can (15 oz) black beans, drained and rinsed
- 1 cup corn kernels (fresh or frozen)
- 1 tsp cumin
- 1 tsp chili powder
- Salt and pepper, to taste
- 1 cup shredded cheese (optional)

Instructions

1. **Prepare the Quinoa:**
    - Rinse the quinoa under cold water. In a medium saucepan, bring vegetable broth (or water) to a boil. Add the quinoa, reduce heat to low, cover, and simmer for about 15 minutes until the quinoa is cooked and the liquid is absorbed. Set aside.
2. **Prepare the Peppers:**
    - Preheat the oven to 375°F (190°C).
    - Slice the tops off the bell peppers and remove the seeds. Place the peppers in a baking dish.
3. **Make the Filling:**
    - Heat olive oil in a pan over medium heat. Add diced onion and garlic and sauté for 3-4 minutes until softened.
    - Add the black beans, corn, cumin, chili powder, salt, and pepper. Stir to combine and cook for another 5 minutes.
    - Stir in the cooked quinoa and mix until well combined.
4. **Stuff the Peppers:**
    - Spoon the quinoa mixture into the hollowed-out peppers, pressing gently to pack the filling.
    - If using cheese, sprinkle it on top of each stuffed pepper.
5. **Bake:**

- Cover the baking dish with foil and bake for 25-30 minutes until the peppers are tender.
- If using cheese, remove the foil during the last 5 minutes to melt the cheese.

Gluten-Free Chicken Alfredo

Ingredients

- 2 tbsp olive oil
- 2 boneless, skinless chicken breasts, cut into strips
- Salt and pepper, to taste
- 2 cups gluten-free pasta (such as fettuccine)
- 1 cup heavy cream
- 1 cup grated Parmesan cheese
- 2 tbsp butter
- 2 garlic cloves, minced
- Fresh parsley, chopped (for garnish)

Instructions

1. **Cook the Pasta:**
   - Bring a pot of salted water to a boil and cook the gluten-free pasta according to the package instructions. Drain and set aside.
2. **Cook the Chicken:**
   - In a large skillet, heat olive oil over medium heat. Season chicken strips with salt and pepper.
   - Cook the chicken in the skillet for 5-7 minutes until fully cooked. Remove from the skillet and set aside.
3. **Make the Alfredo Sauce:**
   - In the same skillet, melt butter over medium heat. Add minced garlic and sauté for 1-2 minutes until fragrant.
   - Add the heavy cream and bring to a simmer. Reduce the heat and stir in the Parmesan cheese until the sauce thickens.
4. **Combine:**
   - Add the cooked chicken and pasta to the skillet and toss everything together until well coated with the Alfredo sauce.
5. **Serve:**
   - Garnish with fresh parsley and additional Parmesan cheese if desired.

Zucchini Noodles with Pesto Chicken

Ingredients

- 4 boneless, skinless chicken breasts
- 2 tbsp olive oil
- Salt and pepper, to taste
- 4 zucchinis, spiralized into noodles
- 1 cup fresh basil leaves
- ¼ cup pine nuts
- 2 garlic cloves
- ½ cup olive oil
- ¼ cup grated Parmesan cheese
- 1 tbsp lemon juice

Instructions

1. **Cook the Chicken:**
    - Heat olive oil in a skillet over medium heat. Season chicken breasts with salt and pepper.
    - Cook for 6-7 minutes per side until the chicken is fully cooked. Set aside to rest before slicing.
2. **Make the Pesto:**
    - In a food processor, combine basil, pine nuts, garlic, olive oil, Parmesan cheese, and lemon juice. Blend until smooth. Adjust seasoning with salt and pepper.
3. **Prepare the Zucchini Noodles:**
    - In a large skillet, sauté the zucchini noodles in olive oil over medium heat for 3-4 minutes until tender but still firm.
4. **Serve:**
    - Toss the zucchini noodles with the pesto sauce. Top with sliced chicken and additional Parmesan cheese if desired.

Sweet Potato and Black Bean Enchiladas

Ingredients

- 2 large sweet potatoes, peeled and diced
- 1 tbsp olive oil
- Salt and pepper, to taste
- 1 can (15 oz) black beans, drained and rinsed
- 1 tsp cumin
- 1 tsp chili powder
- 8 corn tortillas
- 1 cup enchilada sauce
- 1 ½ cups shredded cheese (optional)
- Fresh cilantro, for garnish

Instructions

1. **Roast the Sweet Potatoes:**
   - Preheat the oven to 400°F (200°C). Toss diced sweet potatoes with olive oil, salt, and pepper, then spread them on a baking sheet.
   - Roast for 20-25 minutes until tender and slightly crispy.
2. **Prepare the Filling:**
   - In a bowl, combine the roasted sweet potatoes, black beans, cumin, and chili powder.
3. **Assemble the Enchiladas:**
   - Preheat the oven to 375°F (190°C).
   - Warm the tortillas in the microwave or on a skillet. Spoon the sweet potato and black bean mixture onto each tortilla and roll them up.
   - Place the enchiladas in a baking dish, seam side down. Pour the enchilada sauce over the top and sprinkle with cheese if using.
4. **Bake:**
   - Cover with foil and bake for 20 minutes. Remove the foil during the last 5 minutes to melt the cheese.
5. **Serve:**
   - Garnish with fresh cilantro and serve.

Grilled Salmon with Mango Salsa

Ingredients

- 4 salmon fillets
- 1 tbsp olive oil
- Salt and pepper, to taste
- 1 mango, peeled and diced
- 1 red bell pepper, diced
- 1 small red onion, diced
- 1 tbsp fresh cilantro, chopped
- 1 tbsp lime juice

Instructions

1. **Prepare the Salsa:**
   - In a bowl, combine mango, bell pepper, red onion, cilantro, and lime juice. Season with salt and pepper. Set aside.
2. **Grill the Salmon:**
   - Preheat the grill to medium-high heat. Brush the salmon fillets with olive oil and season with salt and pepper.
   - Grill the salmon for 4-6 minutes per side, depending on thickness, until cooked through.
3. **Serve:**
   - Top the grilled salmon with the fresh mango salsa and serve immediately.

Spaghetti Squash Primavera

Ingredients

- 1 medium spaghetti squash
- 2 tbsp olive oil
- 1 small onion, diced
- 2 garlic cloves, minced
- 1 bell pepper, diced
- 1 zucchini, sliced
- 1 cup cherry tomatoes, halved
- 1 tsp dried oregano
- 1 tsp dried basil
- Salt and pepper, to taste
- Fresh basil for garnish

Instructions

1. **Prepare the Spaghetti Squash:**
   - Preheat the oven to 400°F (200°C). Cut the squash in half lengthwise and scoop out the seeds.
   - Drizzle with olive oil, season with salt and pepper, and roast cut side down on a baking sheet for 30-35 minutes until tender.
2. **Make the Primavera:**
   - In a skillet, heat olive oil over medium heat. Sauté onion, garlic, bell pepper, and zucchini for 5-7 minutes until tender.
   - Add the cherry tomatoes, oregano, basil, salt, and pepper, cooking for an additional 2 minutes.
3. **Assemble:**
   - Use a fork to shred the spaghetti squash into noodles.
   - Toss the squash noodles with the vegetable mixture, and garnish with fresh basil.

Beef and Vegetable Stir-Fry

Ingredients

- 1 lb beef sirloin or flank steak, thinly sliced
- 2 tbsp soy sauce (or tamari for gluten-free)
- 1 tbsp sesame oil
- 1 tbsp olive oil
- 1 bell pepper, sliced
- 1 small broccoli crown, chopped
- 1 carrot, sliced
- 2 garlic cloves, minced
- 1 tbsp ginger, grated
- 1 tbsp honey or maple syrup
- Cooked rice, for serving

Instructions

1. **Prepare the Beef:**
    - In a bowl, marinate the sliced beef with soy sauce and sesame oil for 15-20 minutes.
2. **Stir-Fry the Vegetables:**
    - Heat olive oil in a large skillet over medium-high heat. Add the bell pepper, broccoli, and carrot, and stir-fry for 5-7 minutes until tender.
3. **Cook the Beef:**
    - Push the vegetables to the side of the skillet and add the beef, cooking for 3-4 minutes until browned.
4. **Make the Sauce:**
    - Add garlic, ginger, and honey to the skillet, stirring to combine. Cook for 2 minutes until fragrant.
5. **Serve:**
    - Serve the stir-fry over cooked rice and enjoy!

Chicken Parmesan with Gluten-Free Breadcrumbs

Ingredients

- 4 boneless, skinless chicken breasts
- 1 cup gluten-free breadcrumbs
- 1/2 cup grated Parmesan cheese
- 1 tsp dried oregano
- 1 tsp dried basil
- 2 eggs, beaten
- 2 cups marinara sauce
- 1 1/2 cups shredded mozzarella cheese
- Olive oil, for frying
- Salt and pepper, to taste

Instructions

1. **Prepare the Chicken:**
    - Preheat the oven to 375°F (190°C). Season the chicken breasts with salt and pepper.
    - In a shallow bowl, mix the gluten-free breadcrumbs, Parmesan, oregano, and basil.
    - Dip each chicken breast into the beaten eggs, then coat with the breadcrumb mixture, pressing gently to adhere.
2. **Cook the Chicken:**
    - Heat olive oil in a large skillet over medium heat. Cook the chicken breasts for 4-5 minutes per side until golden brown. Transfer to a baking dish.
3. **Assemble:**
    - Spoon marinara sauce over each chicken breast. Sprinkle with mozzarella cheese.
4. **Bake:**
    - Bake in the oven for 20-25 minutes, or until the chicken is cooked through and the cheese is melted and bubbly.

Eggplant Parmesan

Ingredients

- 2 medium eggplants, sliced into 1/4-inch thick rounds
- 1 1/2 cups gluten-free breadcrumbs
- 1/2 cup grated Parmesan cheese
- 2 eggs, beaten
- 2 cups marinara sauce
- 1 1/2 cups shredded mozzarella cheese
- Olive oil, for frying
- Salt and pepper, to taste

Instructions

1. **Prepare the Eggplant:**
   - Preheat the oven to 375°F (190°C). Sprinkle the eggplant slices with salt and let them sit for 10 minutes to draw out excess moisture, then pat dry with paper towels.
2. **Bread the Eggplant:**
   - In a shallow bowl, combine the gluten-free breadcrumbs and Parmesan. Dip each eggplant slice in the beaten eggs, then coat with the breadcrumb mixture.
3. **Fry the Eggplant:**
   - Heat olive oil in a large skillet over medium heat. Fry the eggplant slices in batches, cooking for 2-3 minutes per side until golden brown. Transfer to a paper towel-lined plate.
4. **Assemble:**
   - In a baking dish, layer the fried eggplant slices, marinara sauce, and mozzarella cheese. Repeat the layers until all ingredients are used.
5. **Bake:**
   - Bake for 25-30 minutes until the cheese is melted and bubbly.

Baked Lemon Garlic Shrimp

Ingredients

- 1 lb large shrimp, peeled and deveined
- 3 tbsp olive oil
- 3 garlic cloves, minced
- 1 tbsp lemon juice
- 1 tsp lemon zest
- 1 tsp dried parsley
- Salt and pepper, to taste
- Fresh parsley, for garnish

Instructions

1. **Preheat the Oven:**
   - Preheat the oven to 400°F (200°C). Arrange the shrimp in a single layer on a baking sheet.
2. **Prepare the Sauce:**
   - In a small bowl, mix the olive oil, garlic, lemon juice, lemon zest, parsley, salt, and pepper.
3. **Bake the Shrimp:**
   - Pour the garlic-lemon mixture over the shrimp and toss to coat. Bake for 8-10 minutes, or until the shrimp are pink and opaque.
4. **Serve:**
   - Garnish with fresh parsley and serve immediately.

Gluten-Free Meatballs with Marinara

Ingredients

- 1 lb ground beef or turkey
- 1/2 cup gluten-free breadcrumbs
- 1/4 cup grated Parmesan cheese
- 1 egg
- 2 garlic cloves, minced
- 1 tbsp dried oregano
- 1 tbsp dried basil
- Salt and pepper, to taste
- 2 cups marinara sauce

Instructions

1. **Preheat the Oven:**
    - Preheat the oven to 375°F (190°C). Line a baking sheet with parchment paper.
2. **Make the Meatballs:**
    - In a large bowl, combine ground meat, gluten-free breadcrumbs, Parmesan, egg, garlic, oregano, basil, salt, and pepper. Mix until well combined.
    - Shape the mixture into meatballs, about 1 1/2 inches in diameter, and place them on the prepared baking sheet.
3. **Bake the Meatballs:**
    - Bake for 20-25 minutes, or until the meatballs are browned and cooked through.
4. **Simmer in Marinara Sauce:**
    - Heat marinara sauce in a large pan over medium heat. Add the baked meatballs and simmer for 10-15 minutes to absorb the flavors.

Grilled Steak with Avocado Salsa

Ingredients

- 2 ribeye or flank steaks
- Salt and pepper, to taste
- 2 ripe avocados, diced
- 1/2 red onion, finely diced
- 1/2 cup cherry tomatoes, halved
- 1 tbsp lime juice
- 1 tbsp cilantro, chopped

Instructions

1. **Grill the Steaks:**
    - Preheat the grill to medium-high heat. Season the steaks with salt and pepper.
    - Grill the steaks for 4-5 minutes per side for medium-rare, or longer for your desired doneness. Let rest for a few minutes.
2. **Make the Salsa:**
    - In a bowl, combine diced avocados, red onion, cherry tomatoes, lime juice, and cilantro. Season with salt and pepper.
3. **Serve:**
    - Slice the grilled steaks and top with the avocado salsa. Serve immediately.

Cauliflower Fried Rice

Ingredients

- 1 medium head cauliflower, grated or processed into rice-sized pieces
- 2 tbsp olive oil
- 1 small onion, diced
- 1 cup frozen peas and carrots
- 2 garlic cloves, minced
- 2 eggs, scrambled
- 3 tbsp gluten-free soy sauce or tamari
- 1 tbsp sesame oil
- Green onions, for garnish

Instructions

1. **Prepare the Cauliflower Rice:**
   - Grate the cauliflower using a box grater or pulse in a food processor until it resembles rice grains.
2. **Cook the Vegetables:**
   - Heat olive oil in a large skillet over medium heat. Add onion and cook for 3-4 minutes until softened.
   - Add peas, carrots, and garlic, and sauté for another 2-3 minutes.
3. **Scramble the Eggs:**
   - Push the vegetables to the side of the skillet and scramble the eggs in the same pan until cooked through.
4. **Fry the Rice:**
   - Add the cauliflower rice to the skillet and stir to combine. Cook for 5-7 minutes, stirring occasionally until tender.
   - Stir in the gluten-free soy sauce and sesame oil, and cook for an additional 2 minutes.
5. **Serve:**
   - Garnish with green onions and serve.

Spaghetti with Ground Turkey and Tomato Sauce

Ingredients

- 1 lb ground turkey
- 1 tbsp olive oil
- 1 onion, diced
- 2 garlic cloves, minced
- 1 can (15 oz) crushed tomatoes
- 1 tbsp dried basil
- 1 tbsp dried oregano
- Salt and pepper, to taste
- 8 oz gluten-free spaghetti

Instructions

1. **Cook the Pasta:**
    - Cook the gluten-free spaghetti according to the package instructions. Drain and set aside.
2. **Make the Sauce:**
    - In a large skillet, heat olive oil over medium heat. Add the ground turkey and cook until browned.
    - Add diced onion and garlic, and cook for 3-4 minutes until softened.
    - Stir in the crushed tomatoes, basil, oregano, salt, and pepper. Simmer for 15-20 minutes to allow the flavors to meld.
3. **Serve:**
    - Toss the cooked spaghetti with the turkey sauce. Serve with additional Parmesan if desired.

Grilled Portobello Mushrooms with Balsamic Glaze

Ingredients

- 4 large Portobello mushroom caps, stems removed
- 2 tbsp olive oil
- 2 tbsp balsamic vinegar
- 1 tbsp honey
- 1 garlic clove, minced
- Salt and pepper, to taste
- Fresh basil, for garnish

Instructions

1. **Prepare the Mushrooms:**
    - Preheat the grill to medium heat. Brush the mushroom caps with olive oil and season with salt and pepper.
2. **Grill the Mushrooms:**
    - Grill the mushrooms for 4-5 minutes per side, until tender.
3. **Make the Balsamic Glaze:**
    - In a small saucepan, combine balsamic vinegar, honey, and minced garlic. Simmer over low heat for 5-7 minutes, until thickened.
4. **Serve:**
    - Drizzle the balsamic glaze over the grilled mushrooms and garnish with fresh basil. Serve immediately.

Gluten-Free Chicken and Rice Casserole

Ingredients

- 2 cups cooked chicken, shredded
- 1 1/2 cups cooked white or brown rice
- 1 can (10 oz) gluten-free cream of mushroom soup
- 1 cup shredded cheddar cheese
- 1/2 cup milk (dairy or dairy-free)
- 1/2 cup chicken broth
- 1/2 cup frozen peas
- 1/2 cup chopped carrots
- 1 small onion, diced
- Salt and pepper, to taste
- 1/2 tsp garlic powder
- 1/2 tsp dried thyme

Instructions

1. **Preheat the Oven:**
   - Preheat your oven to 375°F (190°C) and grease a 9x13-inch baking dish.
2. **Prepare the Casserole:**
   - In a large mixing bowl, combine shredded chicken, cooked rice, cream of mushroom soup, cheddar cheese, milk, chicken broth, peas, carrots, and onion. Season with salt, pepper, garlic powder, and thyme.
3. **Assemble:**
   - Pour the mixture into the prepared baking dish and spread evenly.
4. **Bake:**
   - Cover with aluminum foil and bake for 20-25 minutes. Remove foil, stir the casserole, and bake uncovered for an additional 10-15 minutes until bubbly and golden.

Sweet Potato Gnocchi

Ingredients

- 2 medium sweet potatoes, peeled and cubed
- 1 1/2 cups gluten-free all-purpose flour, plus more for dusting
- 1 egg, lightly beaten
- 1/2 tsp salt
- 1/4 tsp ground nutmeg
- 1 tbsp olive oil (for sautéing)

Instructions

1. **Cook the Sweet Potatoes:**
   - Steam or boil the sweet potato cubes until tender, about 10-12 minutes. Mash the sweet potatoes until smooth and let them cool slightly.
2. **Make the Dough:**
   - In a large bowl, combine the mashed sweet potatoes, gluten-free flour, egg, salt, and nutmeg. Stir until a dough forms. Add more flour if necessary to achieve a smooth, slightly sticky dough.
3. **Form the Gnocchi:**
   - Roll the dough into long ropes on a lightly floured surface and cut into 1-inch pieces. Use a fork to gently press each piece to form the classic gnocchi shape.
4. **Cook the Gnocchi:**
   - Bring a large pot of salted water to a boil. Add the gnocchi in batches. When they float to the surface, cook for an additional 1-2 minutes. Remove with a slotted spoon.
5. **Serve:**
   - Heat olive oil in a pan and sauté the cooked gnocchi for 2-3 minutes until golden and crispy. Serve with your favorite sauce.

Spicy Shrimp Tacos with Lime Crema

Ingredients

- 1 lb large shrimp, peeled and deveined
- 1 tbsp olive oil
- 1 tsp chili powder
- 1 tsp smoked paprika
- 1/2 tsp cumin
- 1/4 tsp cayenne pepper
- Salt and pepper, to taste
- 8 small gluten-free tortillas
- 1/2 cup shredded cabbage (for topping)
- 1/4 cup fresh cilantro, chopped (for topping)

For the Lime Crema:

- 1/2 cup sour cream or Greek yogurt
- 1 tbsp lime juice
- 1 tsp lime zest
- Salt and pepper, to taste

Instructions

1. **Make the Lime Crema:**
   - In a small bowl, combine sour cream, lime juice, lime zest, salt, and pepper. Stir to combine and set aside.
2. **Prepare the Shrimp:**
   - In a bowl, toss the shrimp with olive oil, chili powder, smoked paprika, cumin, cayenne pepper, salt, and pepper.
3. **Cook the Shrimp:**
   - Heat a grill pan or skillet over medium-high heat. Cook the shrimp for 2-3 minutes per side until pink and cooked through.
4. **Assemble the Tacos:**
   - Warm the tortillas in a dry skillet. Divide the cooked shrimp among the tortillas and top with shredded cabbage, cilantro, and a drizzle of lime crema.

Stuffed Acorn Squash with Quinoa and Cranberries

Ingredients

- 2 acorn squash, halved and seeds removed
- 1 tbsp olive oil
- Salt and pepper, to taste
- 1 cup cooked quinoa
- 1/2 cup dried cranberries
- 1/4 cup chopped pecans or walnuts
- 1 tbsp maple syrup
- 1/4 tsp cinnamon
- 1/4 tsp nutmeg
- Fresh parsley, for garnish

Instructions

1. **Prepare the Squash:**
   - Preheat the oven to 375°F (190°C). Brush the cut sides of the acorn squash with olive oil and season with salt and pepper. Place cut-side down on a baking sheet and roast for 30-40 minutes until tender.
2. **Prepare the Filling:**
   - In a medium bowl, combine cooked quinoa, dried cranberries, chopped nuts, maple syrup, cinnamon, and nutmeg. Stir until evenly mixed.
3. **Stuff the Squash:**
   - Once the squash is cooked, remove it from the oven and flip the halves over. Fill each squash half with the quinoa mixture.
4. **Bake:**
   - Return the stuffed squash to the oven and bake for an additional 10-15 minutes to warm through.
5. **Serve:**
   - Garnish with fresh parsley and serve.

Lemon Dill Baked Cod

Ingredients

- 4 cod fillets
- 2 tbsp olive oil
- 1 lemon, thinly sliced
- 1 tbsp fresh dill, chopped
- Salt and pepper, to taste
- 1/2 cup chicken broth

Instructions

1. **Preheat the Oven:**
   - Preheat the oven to 400°F (200°C). Place cod fillets in a baking dish.
2. **Prepare the Cod:**
   - Drizzle the cod fillets with olive oil and season with salt, pepper, and chopped dill. Top each fillet with a few lemon slices.
3. **Bake:**
   - Pour chicken broth around the fish and bake for 12-15 minutes, or until the cod is cooked through and flakes easily with a fork.
4. **Serve:**
   - Serve with additional lemon slices and fresh herbs if desired.

Gluten-Free Beef and Broccoli Stir-Fry

Ingredients

- 1 lb beef sirloin, thinly sliced against the grain
- 2 tbsp gluten-free soy sauce or tamari
- 1 tbsp oyster sauce (optional, check for gluten-free)
- 1 tbsp cornstarch
- 2 tbsp olive oil
- 2 cups broccoli florets
- 1 onion, sliced
- 2 garlic cloves, minced
- 1 tbsp fresh ginger, grated
- 1/4 cup beef broth
- Salt and pepper, to taste

Instructions

1. **Marinate the Beef:**
   - In a bowl, combine the beef slices with soy sauce, oyster sauce (if using), and cornstarch. Toss to coat and set aside for 10-15 minutes.
2. **Cook the Broccoli:**
   - In a large skillet or wok, heat olive oil over medium-high heat. Add broccoli and stir-fry for 3-4 minutes until tender-crisp. Remove from the skillet and set aside.
3. **Stir-Fry the Beef:**
   - In the same skillet, add more olive oil if needed. Add the marinated beef and stir-fry for 2-3 minutes until browned.
4. **Combine:**
   - Add the onion, garlic, and ginger to the pan and cook for another 2-3 minutes. Stir in the beef broth, and cook for an additional 2 minutes until the sauce thickens.
5. **Serve:**
   - Return the broccoli to the pan and toss everything together. Serve hot over rice or quinoa.

Thai Peanut Chicken Stir-Fry

Ingredients

- 1 lb chicken breast, thinly sliced
- 2 tbsp olive oil
- 1 red bell pepper, sliced
- 1 carrot, julienned
- 1 cup snow peas
- 1/4 cup peanut butter (smooth)
- 3 tbsp gluten-free soy sauce or tamari
- 1 tbsp honey
- 1 tbsp rice vinegar
- 1 tsp sesame oil
- 1 garlic clove, minced
- 1 tsp fresh ginger, grated
- Chopped peanuts, for garnish

Instructions

1. **Make the Peanut Sauce:**
   - In a small bowl, whisk together peanut butter, soy sauce, honey, rice vinegar, sesame oil, garlic, and ginger until smooth.
2. **Cook the Chicken:**
   - Heat olive oil in a large skillet over medium-high heat. Add the sliced chicken and cook for 5-6 minutes until browned and cooked through.
3. **Stir-Fry the Vegetables:**
   - Add the bell pepper, carrot, and snow peas to the skillet, and cook for 3-4 minutes until tender-crisp.
4. **Combine:**
   - Pour the peanut sauce over the chicken and vegetables, stirring to coat evenly. Cook for another 2-3 minutes to heat through.
5. **Serve:**
   - Garnish with chopped peanuts and serve with rice or noodles.

Baked Chicken Thighs with Garlic and Herb

Ingredients

- 4 bone-in, skin-on chicken thighs
- 2 tbsp olive oil
- 4 garlic cloves, minced
- 1 tbsp fresh thyme, chopped
- 1 tbsp fresh rosemary, chopped
- 1 lemon, sliced
- Salt and pepper, to taste

Instructions

1. **Preheat the Oven:**
    - Preheat the oven to 425°F (220°C) and line a baking sheet with parchment paper.
2. **Prepare the Chicken:**
    - Rub the chicken thighs with olive oil, minced garlic, fresh thyme, rosemary, salt, and pepper. Place lemon slices around the chicken.
3. **Bake:**
    - Arrange the chicken thighs on the baking sheet and bake for 35-40 minutes, or until the chicken is golden brown and cooked through.
4. **Serve:**
    - Serve with roasted vegetables or a side salad.

Gluten-Free Lasagna with Zucchini Noodles

Ingredients

- 4 large zucchini, sliced into thin strips (zucchini noodles)
- 1 lb ground beef or turkey
- 1 onion, diced
- 2 garlic cloves, minced
- 1 can (14.5 oz) crushed tomatoes
- 1 can (6 oz) tomato paste
- 1 tsp dried basil
- 1 tsp dried oregano
- 1/2 tsp salt
- 1/4 tsp black pepper
- 1/2 tsp red pepper flakes (optional)
- 1 cup ricotta cheese
- 1 cup shredded mozzarella cheese
- 1/2 cup grated Parmesan cheese
- 1 egg
- 1 tbsp olive oil
- Fresh basil, for garnish

Instructions

1. **Prepare the Zucchini Noodles:**
   - Preheat the oven to 375°F (190°C). Slice the zucchini into thin strips using a mandolin or vegetable peeler. Lay the zucchini noodles on paper towels to absorb excess moisture.
2. **Cook the Meat Sauce:**
   - In a large skillet, heat olive oil over medium heat. Add the ground meat, onion, and garlic. Cook until the meat is browned and the onion is tender. Stir in the crushed tomatoes, tomato paste, basil, oregano, salt, pepper, and red pepper flakes. Simmer for 15-20 minutes, stirring occasionally.
3. **Prepare the Ricotta Mixture:**
   - In a bowl, combine ricotta cheese, egg, half of the mozzarella cheese, and Parmesan. Season with a pinch of salt and pepper.
4. **Assemble the Lasagna:**
   - Spread a thin layer of the meat sauce on the bottom of a baking dish. Layer with zucchini noodles, then spread a layer of ricotta mixture. Repeat

the layers until all ingredients are used, finishing with a layer of meat sauce. Top with the remaining mozzarella cheese.
5. **Bake:**
    - Cover with aluminum foil and bake for 20-25 minutes. Remove the foil and bake for another 10-15 minutes, until bubbly and golden.
6. **Serve:**
    - Let the lasagna rest for 5 minutes before serving. Garnish with fresh basil.

Roasted Vegetable and Chickpea Buddha Bowl

Ingredients

- 1 cup cooked quinoa or brown rice
- 1 cup chickpeas, drained and rinsed
- 1 red bell pepper, chopped
- 1 zucchini, chopped
- 1 sweet potato, peeled and cubed
- 1 cup broccoli florets
- 2 tbsp olive oil
- 1 tsp smoked paprika
- 1 tsp ground cumin
- Salt and pepper, to taste
- 2 tbsp tahini
- 1 tbsp lemon juice
- 1 tsp maple syrup
- 1/4 cup water (to thin the dressing)
- Fresh cilantro, for garnish

Instructions

1. **Roast the Vegetables:**
   - Preheat the oven to 400°F (200°C). On a baking sheet, toss the sweet potato, bell pepper, zucchini, and broccoli with olive oil, smoked paprika, cumin, salt, and pepper. Roast for 20-25 minutes, stirring halfway through, until vegetables are tender and lightly browned.
2. **Cook the Chickpeas:**
   - In a small skillet, heat a little olive oil over medium heat. Add the chickpeas and cook for 5-7 minutes until they're golden and crispy. Season with salt and pepper.
3. **Make the Dressing:**
   - In a small bowl, whisk together tahini, lemon juice, maple syrup, and water until smooth.
4. **Assemble the Bowl:**
   - To assemble, start with a base of quinoa or brown rice. Top with roasted vegetables, crispy chickpeas, and drizzle with tahini dressing. Garnish with fresh cilantro.

Salmon and Avocado Rice Bowl

Ingredients

- 2 salmon fillets
- 1 tbsp olive oil
- Salt and pepper, to taste
- 1 cup cooked jasmine or brown rice
- 1 ripe avocado, sliced
- 1 cucumber, thinly sliced
- 1 small carrot, julienned
- 2 tbsp soy sauce or tamari (for gluten-free)
- 1 tsp sesame oil
- 1 tbsp rice vinegar
- 1 tsp honey
- 1 tbsp sesame seeds
- Fresh cilantro, for garnish

Instructions

1. **Cook the Salmon:**
   - Heat olive oil in a skillet over medium heat. Season the salmon fillets with salt and pepper. Cook the salmon for 4-5 minutes per side, until golden brown and cooked through. Remove from heat and flake the salmon with a fork.
2. **Make the Dressing:**
   - In a small bowl, whisk together soy sauce, sesame oil, rice vinegar, and honey.
3. **Assemble the Bowl:**
   - To assemble, place a scoop of rice in each bowl. Top with flaked salmon, avocado slices, cucumber, and carrot. Drizzle with the dressing and sprinkle with sesame seeds and fresh cilantro.

Cauliflower and Chickpea Curry

Ingredients

- 1 tbsp olive oil
- 1 onion, diced
- 2 garlic cloves, minced
- 1 tbsp fresh ginger, grated
- 1 tbsp curry powder
- 1/2 tsp ground cumin
- 1 can (14 oz) diced tomatoes
- 1 can (14 oz) coconut milk
- 1 small cauliflower, cut into florets
- 1 can (15 oz) chickpeas, drained and rinsed
- Salt and pepper, to taste
- Fresh cilantro, for garnish

Instructions

1. **Cook the Aromatics:**
   - Heat olive oil in a large pot over medium heat. Add the onion and cook for 5-7 minutes until soft. Add the garlic and ginger and cook for another minute.
2. **Add Spices:**
   - Stir in the curry powder and cumin, cooking for 1 minute until fragrant.
3. **Simmer the Curry:**
   - Add the diced tomatoes, coconut milk, cauliflower florets, and chickpeas. Stir to combine. Bring to a simmer and cook for 20-25 minutes, until the cauliflower is tender.
4. **Season:**
   - Season with salt and pepper to taste. Garnish with fresh cilantro before serving.

Grilled Chicken with Greek Salad

Ingredients

- 2 chicken breasts
- 1 tbsp olive oil
- 1 tsp dried oregano
- Salt and pepper, to taste
- 1 cucumber, chopped
- 1 cup cherry tomatoes, halved
- 1/2 red onion, thinly sliced
- 1/4 cup Kalamata olives, pitted
- 1/4 cup feta cheese, crumbled
- 2 tbsp olive oil (for salad dressing)
- 1 tbsp red wine vinegar
- 1 tsp dried oregano
- Fresh parsley, for garnish

Instructions

1. **Grill the Chicken:**
    - Preheat the grill or grill pan to medium-high heat. Brush the chicken breasts with olive oil, then season with oregano, salt, and pepper. Grill the chicken for 6-7 minutes per side until fully cooked and internal temperature reaches 165°F (74°C).
2. **Prepare the Salad:**
    - In a large bowl, combine cucumber, cherry tomatoes, red onion, olives, and feta. Toss with olive oil, red wine vinegar, and oregano. Season with salt and pepper.
3. **Serve:**
    - Slice the grilled chicken and serve it on top of the Greek salad. Garnish with fresh parsley.

Eggplant and Spinach Stuffed Chicken

Ingredients

- 2 chicken breasts, boneless and skinless
- 1 eggplant, diced
- 1 tbsp olive oil
- 1 garlic clove, minced
- 2 cups fresh spinach, chopped
- 1/2 cup ricotta cheese
- 1/4 cup mozzarella cheese, shredded
- Salt and pepper, to taste
- 1 tbsp fresh basil, chopped

Instructions

1. **Prepare the Chicken:**
    - Preheat the oven to 375°F (190°C). Cut a pocket into each chicken breast, being careful not to cut all the way through.
2. **Cook the Eggplant and Spinach:**
    - In a skillet, heat olive oil over medium heat. Add diced eggplant and cook for 5-7 minutes until soft. Add garlic and spinach, cooking until the spinach wilts. Remove from heat and stir in ricotta, mozzarella, salt, and pepper.
3. **Stuff the Chicken:**
    - Stuff each chicken breast with the eggplant and spinach mixture, then secure with toothpicks.
4. **Cook the Chicken:**
    - Heat a skillet with olive oil over medium-high heat. Sear each stuffed chicken breast for 2-3 minutes per side, until golden. Transfer to the oven and bake for 20-25 minutes until the chicken is cooked through.
5. **Serve:**
    - Remove toothpicks and serve garnished with fresh basil.

Grilled Shrimp Skewers with Garlic and Lemon

Ingredients

- 1 lb large shrimp, peeled and deveined
- 2 tbsp olive oil
- 3 garlic cloves, minced
- 1 tbsp lemon juice
- 1 tsp lemon zest
- Salt and pepper, to taste
- Fresh parsley, chopped, for garnish

Instructions

1. **Marinate the Shrimp:**
   - In a bowl, combine olive oil, garlic, lemon juice, lemon zest, salt, and pepper. Add the shrimp and toss to coat. Marinate for 15-20 minutes.
2. **Grill the Shrimp:**
   - Preheat the grill to medium-high heat. Thread the shrimp onto skewers. Grill for 2-3 minutes per side until shrimp are pink and cooked through.
3. **Serve:**
   - Remove the shrimp from the skewers and garnish with fresh parsley. Serve with a side of rice or vegetables.

Butternut Squash and Spinach Risotto

Ingredients

- 1 cup Arborio rice
- 2 tbsp olive oil
- 1/2 onion, chopped
- 2 cups butternut squash, cubed
- 3 cups vegetable broth
- 1/2 cup dry white wine
- 2 cups fresh spinach, chopped
- 1/4 cup grated Parmesan cheese
- Salt and pepper, to taste

Instructions

1. **Cook the Butternut Squash:**
    - Preheat the oven to 400°F (200°C). Toss the cubed butternut squash with olive oil, salt, and pepper, and roast for 20-25 minutes until tender.
2. **Cook the Risotto:**
    - In a large pan, heat olive oil over medium heat. Add the onion and cook until soft. Add the Arborio rice and cook for 1-2 minutes. Pour in the white wine and cook until absorbed. Gradually add the vegetable broth, one ladle at a time, stirring constantly until the rice is cooked and creamy, about 18-20 minutes.
3. **Combine:**
    - Stir in the roasted butternut squash, spinach, and Parmesan cheese. Season with salt and pepper to taste.
4. **Serve:**
    - Serve warm as a comforting side dish or light main course.

Gluten-Free Shrimp Scampi

Ingredients

- 1 lb large shrimp, peeled and deveined
- 12 oz gluten-free pasta (such as spaghetti or linguine)
- 3 tbsp olive oil
- 4 garlic cloves, minced
- 1/2 tsp red pepper flakes (optional)
- 1/2 cup dry white wine
- 1/4 cup fresh lemon juice
- 1/4 cup fresh parsley, chopped
- Salt and pepper, to taste
- Zest of 1 lemon

Instructions

1. **Cook the Pasta:**
    - Cook the gluten-free pasta according to the package instructions. Drain and set aside, reserving some pasta water.
2. **Cook the Shrimp:**
    - In a large skillet, heat olive oil over medium heat. Add the shrimp and cook for 2-3 minutes per side until pink and cooked through. Remove the shrimp from the skillet and set aside.
3. **Make the Scampi Sauce:**
    - In the same skillet, add garlic and red pepper flakes, cooking for 1 minute until fragrant. Add the white wine and lemon juice, scraping the bottom of the skillet to release any browned bits. Simmer for 3-4 minutes until the sauce slightly reduces.
4. **Combine:**
    - Return the shrimp to the skillet, along with the cooked pasta. Toss to combine, adding a bit of reserved pasta water if needed to create a silky sauce. Season with salt, pepper, and lemon zest.
5. **Serve:**
    - Garnish with fresh parsley and serve immediately.

Chicken and Vegetable Skewers

Ingredients

- 2 boneless, skinless chicken breasts, cut into cubes
- 1 red bell pepper, cut into chunks
- 1 zucchini, sliced
- 1 yellow onion, cut into chunks
- 1 cup cherry tomatoes
- 2 tbsp olive oil
- 1 tbsp lemon juice
- 1 tsp dried oregano
- Salt and pepper, to taste
- Wooden skewers (soaked in water for 30 minutes)

Instructions

1. **Prepare the Marinade:**
   - In a bowl, mix olive oil, lemon juice, oregano, salt, and pepper. Add the chicken cubes and marinate for at least 15 minutes.
2. **Assemble the Skewers:**
   - Preheat the grill to medium-high heat. Thread the marinated chicken, bell pepper, zucchini, onion, and cherry tomatoes onto the skewers, alternating between the ingredients.
3. **Grill:**
   - Grill the skewers for 10-12 minutes, turning occasionally, until the chicken is cooked through and the vegetables are tender.
4. **Serve:**
   - Remove from the grill and serve immediately.

Spaghetti with Gluten-Free Meat Sauce

Ingredients

- 12 oz gluten-free spaghetti
- 1 lb ground beef or turkey
- 1 onion, chopped
- 2 garlic cloves, minced
- 1 can (14.5 oz) crushed tomatoes
- 1 can (6 oz) tomato paste
- 1 tsp dried basil
- 1 tsp dried oregano
- 1/4 tsp salt
- 1/4 tsp black pepper
- 1/2 cup grated Parmesan cheese (optional)

Instructions

1. **Cook the Pasta:**
    - Cook the gluten-free spaghetti according to the package instructions. Drain and set aside.
2. **Make the Meat Sauce:**
    - In a large skillet, cook the ground meat over medium heat, breaking it up as it cooks. Once browned, add the onion and garlic, cooking until softened, about 5 minutes. Stir in the crushed tomatoes, tomato paste, basil, oregano, salt, and pepper. Simmer for 15-20 minutes, stirring occasionally.
3. **Combine:**
    - Toss the cooked spaghetti with the meat sauce, adding a little reserved pasta water to thin the sauce if necessary.
4. **Serve:**
    - Top with grated Parmesan cheese (if using) and serve immediately.

Baked Parmesan Crusted Tilapia

Ingredients

- 4 tilapia fillets
- 1/2 cup gluten-free breadcrumbs
- 1/2 cup grated Parmesan cheese
- 1 tsp garlic powder
- 1/2 tsp dried basil
- 1/2 tsp dried oregano
- Salt and pepper, to taste
- 1 egg, beaten
- 2 tbsp olive oil

Instructions

1. **Prepare the Coating:**
   - Preheat the oven to 375°F (190°C). In a shallow bowl, mix together the gluten-free breadcrumbs, Parmesan, garlic powder, basil, oregano, salt, and pepper.
2. **Coat the Tilapia:**
   - Dip each tilapia fillet into the beaten egg, then dredge in the breadcrumb mixture, pressing gently to coat.
3. **Bake:**
   - Place the coated tilapia fillets on a baking sheet lined with parchment paper. Drizzle with olive oil and bake for 12-15 minutes, or until the fish flakes easily with a fork.
4. **Serve:**
   - Serve the baked tilapia with a side of your favorite vegetables or a salad.

Gluten-Free Beef Tacos with Avocado

Ingredients

- 1 lb ground beef
- 1 packet gluten-free taco seasoning (or homemade seasoning)
- 1/2 cup water
- 8 gluten-free taco shells
- 1 avocado, sliced
- 1/2 cup shredded lettuce
- 1/4 cup diced tomatoes
- 1/4 cup shredded cheese (optional)
- 2 tbsp sour cream (optional)
- Fresh cilantro, for garnish

Instructions

1. **Cook the Beef:**
   - In a skillet, cook the ground beef over medium heat until browned. Drain any excess fat. Add the taco seasoning and water, then stir to combine. Simmer for 5 minutes until the sauce thickens.
2. **Prepare the Toppings:**
   - While the beef cooks, slice the avocado, chop the lettuce and tomatoes, and set aside any other desired toppings.
3. **Assemble the Tacos:**
   - Warm the gluten-free taco shells in the oven or microwave. Spoon the beef mixture into each shell, then top with avocado, lettuce, tomatoes, cheese, and sour cream.
4. **Serve:**
   - Garnish with fresh cilantro and serve immediately.

Sweet Potato and Kale Salad

Ingredients

- 2 medium sweet potatoes, peeled and cubed
- 1 tbsp olive oil
- Salt and pepper, to taste
- 4 cups kale, chopped
- 1/4 cup pumpkin seeds
- 1/4 cup dried cranberries
- 1/4 cup feta cheese (optional)
- 2 tbsp balsamic vinegar
- 1 tbsp olive oil

Instructions

1. **Roast the Sweet Potatoes:**
   - Preheat the oven to 400°F (200°C). Toss the cubed sweet potatoes with olive oil, salt, and pepper. Roast for 20-25 minutes, turning halfway through, until tender.
2. **Prepare the Salad:**
   - In a large bowl, massage the chopped kale with olive oil to soften it. Add the roasted sweet potatoes, pumpkin seeds, cranberries, and feta (if using).
3. **Make the Dressing:**
   - In a small bowl, whisk together balsamic vinegar and olive oil. Pour over the salad and toss to combine.
4. **Serve:**
   - Serve the salad warm or at room temperature.

Grilled Veggie and Hummus Wrap

Ingredients

- 1 zucchini, sliced
- 1 red bell pepper, sliced
- 1 yellow bell pepper, sliced
- 1/2 red onion, sliced
- 2 tbsp olive oil
- Salt and pepper, to taste
- 4 gluten-free wraps
- 1/2 cup hummus
- Fresh spinach or arugula (optional)

Instructions

1. **Grill the Vegetables:**
   - Preheat the grill or grill pan to medium-high heat. Toss the zucchini, bell peppers, and onion with olive oil, salt, and pepper. Grill the vegetables for 5-7 minutes, turning occasionally until tender and slightly charred.
2. **Assemble the Wrap:**
   - Spread a layer of hummus on each gluten-free wrap. Top with grilled vegetables and spinach or arugula.
3. **Wrap and Serve:**
   - Roll up the wraps and serve immediately.

Lemon Garlic Chicken with Quinoa

Ingredients

- 2 boneless, skinless chicken breasts
- 2 tbsp olive oil
- 3 garlic cloves, minced
- Juice and zest of 1 lemon
- 1 cup quinoa, rinsed
- 2 cups water or chicken broth
- Salt and pepper, to taste
- Fresh parsley, chopped, for garnish

Instructions

1. **Prepare the Chicken:**
    - In a small bowl, mix olive oil, garlic, lemon juice, and zest. Season with salt and pepper. Marinate the chicken breasts in the mixture for at least 15 minutes.
2. **Cook the Quinoa:**
    - In a saucepan, bring the water or chicken broth to a boil. Add the quinoa, reduce the heat, and simmer for 15 minutes, until the liquid is absorbed and the quinoa is tender.
3. **Cook the Chicken:**
    - In a skillet, heat a bit of olive oil over medium heat. Cook the chicken for 5-7 minutes per side, until fully cooked.
4. **Serve:**
    - Serve the chicken over the quinoa and garnish with fresh parsley.

Mediterranean Chicken Bowl

Ingredients

- 2 boneless, skinless chicken breasts
- 1 tbsp olive oil
- 1 tsp garlic powder
- 1 tsp dried oregano
- Salt and pepper, to taste
- 1 cup cooked quinoa or rice
- 1/2 cucumber, diced
- 1/2 cup cherry tomatoes, halved
- 1/4 red onion, thinly sliced
- 1/4 cup Kalamata olives, sliced
- 1/4 cup feta cheese, crumbled
- 2 tbsp fresh parsley, chopped
- 2 tbsp tzatziki sauce

Instructions

1. **Cook the Chicken:**
   - Preheat the grill or skillet to medium-high heat. Rub the chicken breasts with olive oil, garlic powder, oregano, salt, and pepper. Cook the chicken for 6-7 minutes per side until fully cooked. Let rest before slicing.
2. **Assemble the Bowl:**
   - In a bowl, layer the quinoa or rice, cucumber, tomatoes, red onion, olives, feta cheese, and parsley.
3. **Top with Chicken:**
   - Slice the cooked chicken and place it on top of the bowl.
4. **Serve:**
   - Drizzle with tzatziki sauce and serve immediately.

Black Bean and Corn Quinoa Salad

Ingredients

- 1 cup quinoa, cooked
- 1 can (15 oz) black beans, drained and rinsed
- 1 cup corn kernels (fresh, frozen, or canned)
- 1 red bell pepper, diced
- 1/4 cup red onion, diced
- 1/4 cup fresh cilantro, chopped
- 1 tbsp lime juice
- 2 tbsp olive oil
- 1 tsp cumin
- Salt and pepper, to taste

Instructions

1. **Prepare the Salad:**
   - In a large bowl, combine the cooked quinoa, black beans, corn, bell pepper, onion, and cilantro.
2. **Make the Dressing:**
   - In a small bowl, whisk together the lime juice, olive oil, cumin, salt, and pepper.
3. **Toss and Serve:**
   - Pour the dressing over the salad and toss until everything is well coated. Serve chilled or at room temperature.

Zucchini and Ground Turkey Lasagna

Ingredients

- 2 large zucchinis, sliced into thin strips
- 1 lb ground turkey
- 1 onion, chopped
- 2 garlic cloves, minced
- 1 can (15 oz) crushed tomatoes
- 1 tbsp tomato paste
- 1 tsp dried oregano
- 1 tsp dried basil
- Salt and pepper, to taste
- 1 1/2 cups ricotta cheese
- 1 cup shredded mozzarella cheese
- 1/4 cup grated Parmesan cheese
- Fresh basil, for garnish

Instructions

1. **Cook the Ground Turkey:**
   - In a large skillet, cook the ground turkey over medium heat until browned. Add the onion and garlic, and cook for 5 minutes until softened. Stir in the crushed tomatoes, tomato paste, oregano, basil, salt, and pepper. Simmer for 10 minutes.
2. **Prepare the Zucchini:**
   - Preheat the oven to 375°F (190°C). Arrange zucchini strips on a baking sheet and roast for 10-15 minutes to release moisture. Pat dry with a paper towel.
3. **Assemble the Lasagna:**
   - In a baking dish, layer zucchini strips, followed by the turkey mixture, ricotta cheese, and mozzarella. Repeat the layers until ingredients are used up. Finish with a layer of mozzarella and Parmesan cheese.
4. **Bake:**
   - Cover with foil and bake for 25 minutes. Remove the foil and bake for an additional 10 minutes until the cheese is golden and bubbly.
5. **Serve:**
   - Garnish with fresh basil and serve.

Sweet Chili Chicken with Vegetables

Ingredients

- 4 boneless, skinless chicken breasts
- 1/4 cup sweet chili sauce
- 2 tbsp soy sauce (or tamari for gluten-free)
- 1 tbsp rice vinegar
- 1 tbsp olive oil
- 1 red bell pepper, sliced
- 1 zucchini, sliced
- 1/2 cup snap peas
- 2 garlic cloves, minced
- Salt and pepper, to taste
- Fresh cilantro, for garnish

Instructions

1. **Marinate the Chicken:**
   - In a bowl, mix the sweet chili sauce, soy sauce, rice vinegar, olive oil, garlic, salt, and pepper. Place the chicken breasts in the marinade and let sit for at least 30 minutes.
2. **Cook the Chicken:**
   - Preheat a grill or skillet over medium heat. Cook the chicken for 6-7 minutes per side until fully cooked. Remove from heat and let rest.
3. **Cook the Vegetables:**
   - In the same skillet, sauté the bell pepper, zucchini, and snap peas for 5-6 minutes until tender.
4. **Serve:**
   - Slice the chicken and serve it over the sautéed vegetables. Garnish with fresh cilantro.

Shrimp and Grits

Ingredients

- 1 lb shrimp, peeled and deveined
- 1 cup grits (gluten-free if needed)
- 2 cups chicken broth
- 1/4 cup heavy cream
- 1 tbsp butter
- 2 tbsp olive oil
- 3 garlic cloves, minced
- 1/2 tsp paprika
- Salt and pepper, to taste
- Fresh parsley, for garnish

Instructions

1. **Cook the Grits:**
   - In a saucepan, bring the chicken broth to a boil. Stir in the grits, reduce the heat, and simmer for 5-7 minutes, stirring occasionally. Once thickened, stir in the heavy cream and butter. Season with salt and pepper.
2. **Cook the Shrimp:**
   - In a large skillet, heat olive oil over medium heat. Add the garlic and sauté for 1 minute. Add the shrimp, paprika, salt, and pepper, cooking for 2-3 minutes per side until pink and cooked through.
3. **Serve:**
   - Spoon the grits onto a plate and top with the shrimp. Garnish with fresh parsley and serve immediately.

Gluten-Free Chicken Enchilada Casserole

Ingredients

- 2 cups cooked chicken, shredded
- 1 can (15 oz) gluten-free enchilada sauce
- 1 cup gluten-free corn tortillas, cut into strips
- 1 can (15 oz) black beans, drained and rinsed
- 1 cup corn kernels (fresh, frozen, or canned)
- 1/2 onion, chopped
- 1 tsp cumin
- 1 tsp chili powder
- 1/2 cup shredded cheddar cheese
- 1/2 cup shredded mozzarella cheese
- 1/4 cup fresh cilantro, chopped
- Salt and pepper, to taste

Instructions

1. **Preheat the Oven:**
    - Preheat your oven to 375°F (190°C). Lightly grease a 9x13-inch baking dish.
2. **Prepare the Filling:**
    - In a large bowl, combine the shredded chicken, black beans, corn, onion, cumin, chili powder, salt, and pepper.
3. **Assemble the Casserole:**
    - Layer the bottom of the baking dish with a few strips of corn tortillas. Top with half of the chicken mixture, then sprinkle with cheddar and mozzarella cheese. Repeat the layers.
4. **Bake:**
    - Cover with foil and bake for 25-30 minutes. Remove the foil and bake for an additional 10-15 minutes until the cheese is bubbly and golden.
5. **Serve:**
    - Garnish with fresh cilantro and serve.

Veggie and Quinoa Stir-Fry

Ingredients

- 1 cup quinoa, cooked
- 1 tbsp olive oil
- 1/2 onion, chopped
- 1 bell pepper, sliced
- 1 zucchini, sliced
- 1 carrot, julienned
- 1 cup snap peas
- 2 garlic cloves, minced
- 2 tbsp soy sauce (or tamari for gluten-free)
- 1 tbsp rice vinegar
- 1 tsp sesame oil
- 1 tbsp sesame seeds (optional)
- Fresh cilantro, for garnish

Instructions

1. **Prepare the Quinoa:**
   - Cook quinoa according to package instructions and set aside.
2. **Stir-Fry the Vegetables:**
   - In a large skillet or wok, heat olive oil over medium heat. Add the onion and cook for 2-3 minutes. Add the bell pepper, zucchini, carrot, and snap peas, and stir-fry for 5-7 minutes until vegetables are tender-crisp.
3. **Combine and Season:**
   - Add the garlic and cook for 1 minute. Stir in the cooked quinoa, soy sauce, rice vinegar, and sesame oil. Toss to combine and heat through.
4. **Serve:**
   - Garnish with sesame seeds and fresh cilantro before serving.

Spaghetti with Gluten-Free Carbonara

Ingredients

- 8 oz gluten-free spaghetti
- 4 slices bacon, chopped
- 2 large eggs
- 1/2 cup grated Parmesan cheese
- 1/2 cup heavy cream
- 1 garlic clove, minced
- Salt and pepper, to taste
- Fresh parsley, for garnish

Instructions

1. **Cook the Spaghetti:**
   - Cook the gluten-free spaghetti according to package instructions. Drain and set aside.
2. **Cook the Bacon:**
   - In a large skillet, cook the chopped bacon over medium heat until crispy. Remove from the skillet and set aside.
3. **Make the Carbonara Sauce:**
   - In a bowl, whisk together the eggs, Parmesan cheese, heavy cream, garlic, salt, and pepper.
4. **Combine:**
   - Add the cooked spaghetti to the skillet with the bacon grease. Pour in the egg mixture and toss quickly to coat the pasta. Add the cooked bacon and continue tossing until the sauce thickens and coats the pasta.
5. **Serve:**
   - Garnish with fresh parsley and more Parmesan cheese if desired.

Baked Tilapia with Herb Butter

Ingredients

- 4 tilapia fillets
- 2 tbsp butter, melted
- 1 tsp garlic powder
- 1 tsp dried thyme
- 1 tsp dried parsley
- 1/2 tsp lemon zest
- Salt and pepper, to taste
- Lemon wedges, for serving

Instructions

1. **Preheat the Oven:**
   - Preheat the oven to 375°F (190°C). Place the tilapia fillets on a baking sheet lined with parchment paper.
2. **Prepare the Herb Butter:**
   - In a small bowl, mix together the melted butter, garlic powder, thyme, parsley, lemon zest, salt, and pepper.
3. **Bake the Tilapia:**
   - Brush the herb butter mixture over the tilapia fillets. Bake for 12-15 minutes or until the fish flakes easily with a fork.
4. **Serve:**
   - Serve the baked tilapia with lemon wedges on the side.

Gluten-Free Stuffed Peppers with Ground Beef

Ingredients

- 4 large bell peppers, tops removed and seeds scooped out
- 1 lb ground beef
- 1/2 onion, chopped
- 1 garlic clove, minced
- 1 cup cooked quinoa or rice
- 1 can (15 oz) diced tomatoes
- 1 tsp cumin
- 1 tsp chili powder
- Salt and pepper, to taste
- 1 cup shredded cheese (cheddar or mozzarella)
- Fresh cilantro, for garnish

Instructions

1. **Prepare the Peppers:**
    - Preheat the oven to 375°F (190°C). Place the bell peppers in a baking dish and bake for 10 minutes to soften.
2. **Cook the Beef Filling:**
    - In a large skillet, cook the ground beef over medium heat until browned. Add the onion and garlic, and cook for another 5 minutes until softened. Stir in the quinoa or rice, diced tomatoes, cumin, chili powder, salt, and pepper. Cook for 5 minutes until heated through.
3. **Stuff the Peppers:**
    - Remove the peppers from the oven. Stuff each bell pepper with the beef mixture and top with shredded cheese.
4. **Bake:**
    - Return the stuffed peppers to the oven and bake for another 10-15 minutes, until the cheese is melted and bubbly.
5. **Serve:**
    - Garnish with fresh cilantro and serve.